imperfections

six broken hearts
&
one red balloon

ryonen yeddo

2018

©

nothing of this world
is mine or yours

we belong far away
from here

maybe
there

the moment
you know
who you are

and
what you need
to be

your true propose
begins

i
wished a hill
but
received
a mountain

i
feel the pain
of climbing
such gift

but

i

am
grateful

the heart hurts
when broken
by the power
of love

or

the weakness
of hate

i
do not do crazy

too crazy
to handle

is
certainly

too crazy
to love

the eternity
of my consciousness
enriches the infinity
of my
realization and existence

i
am
the mystical world
that
i
decided
to
become

never is a long way
from today

....

secrets
are remedies
of brutal
reality

let the rain
bring flowers
and
hide my tears

we mastered love
and
we felt hate

we
laugh and cried

we
existed
together

**Happiness
does not
come alone
where there is
only desire**

i
shaped
happiness

universally

even the shadows
of
unhappiness
transforms
the days

to
uncertain
sadness

play the music
of the gods

and
sit by the fire
completing your puzzle

of
your heart

one by one
created great distance
from others and themselves

i

remain

by my side

i
understand happiness
when
i
feel your smile
and
digest your thoughts

take me
to the moon

and
let me be

i

want to go home

i

want to be free

a red balloon
and
98 others
flew away into the blue sky

we stay
looking at the stars

pondering
when you should depart

all
the imperfections
of the world
are mastered by humanity

and

by our

master

i
desire less than rain

i
seek less than nothing

just because

i
want to endure happiness

one
more time

i
dream of happiness

i
dream of you

so many days passed

and

i
am
still
waiting for you

six
chess moves

combination
promotion
sacrifice
check
checkmate
attack

you
die

our inner selves
are thirsty
for mindful knowledge

knowledge
to be
acknowledged
and
reborn

you make me happy
in the morning
when
the smell of your skin
touches my lips
and
i
purify my thoughts
in your eyes

when
your smile slaves
my hands into your body

and

you
become my ecstasy

my
genuine nature
is to save
is to love
and to care

even
when your nature
is to sting me

earth
does not refuse
seeds

therefore

i
will not refuse
you

create and heal
do not
destroy

remember

you
are not a child

you
are like everyone else
delivering a message
from the universe

the last time
i care this much

i
died

be awake

that
is
what you must be

there is life
after birth

believe

unborn child

i
insist
to love
who hates

and never to hate
who loves

recycle your worries
respect your happiness
eliminate your desires
enjoy enlightenment

you are awake

finally

misery
requires the opposite
of happiness

i

wish

you were happy with me

we are happy
today and tomorrow

because

we
know to be happy
unconditionally

all things
are effects of causes

i
love you

do you love me?

do not judge
never judge

stop judging
based on subjective ideas

the laws of nature
are clear

awareness clarifies
the most foggy
mind

faith
wonder
determination

stay and go
awareness

let
me
tell
you
about
Zen

the ultimate secret
to achieve freedom:

- *do not fear death* -

the one
free from death
was born
free

my fathers' discipline
made me stronger

good
wiser
fair

and
reasonable

if your goal
is to be free

you must study
the nature
of your
cage

the highest wisdom
breaths attention
and
conquers stillness

change your opinions
surrender your speculations
empty your perceptions

then

know
Zen

the fearless attitude
is spontaneous

i
fear
lack of peace

what do you fear?

a frog knows
how a fly tastes

and
a snake knows
how a frog tastes

we
will be
our future
character

some parents
suffer more than others

and
some people
will never

be
parents

i
was obsessed
about you

we
were fourteen

i
eat everyday
chocolate cheesecake with
strawberries

i

am
happy

are you happy?

the voices of nature
speak with me calmly

i

am

at peace

with nature

what brings us together
has more power
than the gods

and
more wisdom
than eternity

what is it?

i
am
accountable
for my actions
and my thoughts

until

i
die

today
nothing matters
more than
the blue sky
reflecting
the rebel waves
of the beach

i
feel sorry
for the broken hearts
drying on the sun
and
the limping star fish

matilda & max
do not love denny
as much

i
love you

it is my intention
to seek light

if
darkness returns

the heavy thoughts passed

i

am

again

with peace

the master sculptor
pursues the perfect stone
to sculptor perfection

i
recognize characters
by the sound of their voices

secret tones of envy
when congratulating

and
tones of satisfaction
when condoling

i
also met
sincere voices

i
know the way
to the mountain
of joy

the path is narrow

there is no desire
there is no hatred
there is no worries
there is no suffering

you
may enter
alone

i
am
a dream of a dream
of
something or someone
dreaming of me

who am i?

focus
on enlightenment

everything else
is exact

stop thinking
and
start walking

said the eagle
to the turtle

patience
does not discriminate

apply it

the world goes
on becoming more beautiful

because
of wise efforts
and
less greed

your tongue has no bone
so you can use it freely

for love
or
for hate

my
heartbeat
is proud of me

i
do not seek
approval or acceptance
from no-one

my
self-realization
is real

we
are the people
practicing the *way*

and
scrabbling wonders

nothing in the world
is hidden

not even
this or that

i
stay in the *now*
waiting for woRLd
to wake up

let me remind you
of the beauty of simplicity

just watch the rain
and the rays of the sun

just feel the sea
and the curves of the wind

just smell the bellis perennis
and touch the earth

just look for you
in what you must be

i
sit in the midst of everything
and
remain stillness

forever
learning everything
that is to know

and
by awaking the status
of curiosity

i
exist
totally

be
genuine in all things
become the best
of you

enjoy
the solitude
and beauty of nature

climb
the highest mountain
you may find

look
at the stars shimmering

understand
the sights
sounds
and smells

and
return home
slowly

set back to comprehend
what you don't understand

you may be too close to see
or too far to acknowledge

set back
again

adjust
to the sun and the rain

like flowers
do

vast emptiness
fulfil enlightenment

not holiness

the power
to change everything
starts with changing
your attitude

perception
commands
imagination

your thoughts
are what you are

and

your thoughts
are what you may become

your thoughts
are simply
you

you
are never defeated
by others

only
by yourself

your
clothes do not make you

but
your attitude
do

let me tell you
about happiness
when you find time
to listen

death
may bring us
to a happy place

and

conclude
physical pain

we
were happier
than we are now

we
were young
impulsive
determined
ambitious
and
in
love

i
am happy
eating eggs

and

i
am happy
feeding chickens

happiness
does not seek itself

do
not let
criticism or praise
disturb or distract
your
heart

keep your mind
clear

illusions
blind us

and
rob us
from ourselves

clarify the mind

and
arrive at your source

a calm and settled mind
will achieve enlightenment
under the sun or the moon

meditate

as much
as permitted

i
instructed you
to be happy

go with the flow

you
will find
your way out
of the mountain

and
back to the sea

happiness
is appropriate
for everyone

even for you
and
me

imagination
art and philosophy
make me happy
or disappointed

the one
who loves the most
suffers the most

i
loved you enough
to understand
that hate has no chance
to conquer
my feelings

we
unconditionally
love
when we are capable
to care
unconditionally

war and love
may seed
predicaments

to love
is to
exist

everywhere

i
hold the universe
in my mind
as much
you
do

do not seek love
until
you are able to handle
storms
springs
and
dreams

when the heart laughs
the heart fears nothing

the benefits of laugher
are not recognized
by miserable people

time is shortened
by age

and
time
determines
my existence

time is an illusion

how much illusion
do you have?

free are the birds
with flying wings

and

no cage

an hour and a second
are from the same time

sometimes

triskele
triskelion

birth
death
rebirth

mystery and promise
a moment on a wheel turns
turns and turns

how much fear would you have
after knowing eternity?